ICONS

Angels

Gilles Néret

TASCHEN

KÖLN LONDON LOS ANGELES MADRID PARIS TOKYO

Contenido | Sommario | Índice

Ángeles puros… ángeles radiantes…

Los ángeles siempre han sido un tema pictórico predilecto entre los artistas, ya que, al estar dotados de alas, es posible colocarlos en cualquier punto del lienzo y en las más diversas posiciones. Así, en el cielo se representan angelitos tocando un sinfín de instrumentos musicales, cantando y danzando. Al crecer se convierten en mensajeros de Dios y cumplen misiones como aparecérsele a la Virgen María con la buena nueva de que lleva en su seno la semilla de Cristo o anunciar a los pastores la venida del Mesías o la llegada de los Reyes Magos de Oriente. Los ángeles de un rango superior, como los arcángeles, pasan a formar parte de la milicia celestial y, desde las nubes, atraviesan con sus lanzas a los demonios… Desde el principio de los tiempos, estos pequeños seres rollizos y sonrientes han sido objeto de un culto particular. En las teogonías más antiguas la figura del ángel se consideraba uno de los elementos primordiales del mundo, una suerte de dios creador nacido del caos primitivo. Para los griegos era *Eros*, el dios que gobernaba los matrimonios y las victorias. A partir del siglo VI a.C. se le otorgó el papel de intermediario entre los dioses y los humanos y se convirtió en la divinidad de la pasión y el amor. Con o sin arco, este espíritu celestial ha sido fuente de inspiración para casi todos los poetas y artistas, quienes lo han mostrado encendiendo los corazones o hiriéndolos con sus flechas. Rebautizado con el nombre de Amor o Cupido por los romanos, Eros conservó el aspecto infantil que le concedió Praxíteles hasta que sus sucesores lo dotaron de rasgos adolescentes. Según parece, fueron los hebreos quienes convirtieron en ángel a este dios menor del amor (del latín *angelus* y del griego *angelos*, que significa «mensajero»), a quien se le ofrecía hospitalidad y la agradecía con bendiciones, promesas de prosperidad y satisfacciones futuras. Con el tiempo, los ángeles pasaron a ser considerados seres inmateriales, se los bautizó con los nombres de las virtudes divinas, y ciertos genios –como los querubines, guardianes de las puertas, y los serafines, serpientes de fuego aladas– ascendieron al reino celestial. Con el advenimiento de la era cristiana, devinieron substancias incorpóreas, inteligentes y superiores al alma de los humanos. La Iglesia enseña que Dios concibió a los ángeles en un estado de bondad y gracia, pero les concedió la libertad de elegir entre el bien y el mal. Algunos de ellos pecaron y fueron condenados a un suplicio infinito. De ahí que existan *ángeles buenos*, los fieles, y *ángeles caídos* o *ángeles malos*, también denominados *diablos* o *demonios*. Aunque la Iglesia recela de los ángeles, varios de ellos aparecen en las Escrituras: Miguel, Gabriel y Rafael entre los buenos, y Satán, Belzebú y otros entre los caídos. El ángel dotado de alas

Sandro Botticelli *The Archangel Gabriel*. Detail of *The Annunciation*, c. 1489.
Florence, Galleria degli Uffizi

nace en el siglo IV, por analogía con las figuras aladas de la Antigüedad. Todo indica que los artistas confundieron a los amorcillos mitológicos con los ángeles y a los serafines con los cupidos… Los ángeles, que hasta la fecha se representaban en actitud hierática, ataviados con túnicas blancas y con expresión de pureza, empezaron entonces a presentar rasgos originales. Con el paso del tiempo, el noble naturalismo del siglo XIII (ángeles de las catedrales) y la suavidad vaporosa de los cuatrocentistas darían paso a una belleza más regular, aunque también más pagana, donde es posible hallar reminiscencias de la Antigüedad. Y por fin Rafael convirtió a estos seres en bellezas serenas. En el Renacimiento se oscilaba, como Tiziano, entre *El amor divino y el amor profano*. Botticelli pintaba temas paganos y sagrados e igual representaba a Venus que a la Virgen María, haciendo que en torno a ambas revolotearan los mismos querubines. Tintoretto, Veronés y Caravaggio se concentraron en *El amor vencido y el amor vencedor*, mientras que Perugino dudaba ante *El combate entre Amor y Castidad*. Rubens, entre los flamencos, fue quien mejor supo entremezclar lo sagrado y lo profano. En Francia, en el siglo XVII, Poussin, y luego Boucher y Fragonard, se encargaron de portar la antorcha que habría de iluminar tanto el amor espiritual como el terrenal. Por desgracia, poco a poco, y sobre todo en la época de los pintores «pompiers», el ángel sonriente fue transformándose en un niño rollizo de celuloide, antes de huir, desfigurado y con las alas hechas jirones, ante la amenaza del arte moderno. Actualmente ha desaparecido de nuestras vidas, ahuyentado por una época que ha perdido la fe en el reino sobrenatural, un reino encantado donde era posible vislumbrar las esencias inmateriales y luminosas de estas graciosas criaturas aladas. Mas, pese a todo, esta imaginería milenaria sigue formando parte de nosotros gracias a los tesoros artísticos cobijados en las iglesias y los museos y a las ingenuas ilustraciones conservadas en las bibliotecas. Hoy más que nunca, los seres humanos se hallan sumidos en el horror de una lucha celestial que les sobrepasa: el combate siempre dudoso entre el Bien y el Mal. En estas representaciones, los ángeles son inseparables de los demonios a los que siempre han estado asociados, tanto en el mundo espiritual como en el arte. Y es que…¿ acaso no son las dos caras de una misma realidad inmaterial? ¿No representan, justamente, una parte de ensueño de esta sociedad excesivamente materialista? «El hombre no es ni ángel ni bestia», afirmó Pascal en el siglo XVII. Hoy, una época en que los ángeles han huido en busca de refugio, podríamos añadir, tal y como reza el dicho popular que «todo ángel tiene algo de demonio»…

Angeli puri… Angeli radiosi…

Agli artisti è sempre piaciuto dipingere gli angeli perché, con le loro ali minute, possono essere raffigurati in qualsiasi punto della tela e anche più volte se così piace. Nel cielo possono suonare una miriade di strumenti musicali, cantare, danzare. Da grandi vengono incaricati di trasportare dei messaggi, come annunciare alla Vergine Maria che è in attesa di un bambino che sarà il Cristo e svelare l'evento ai pastori o ai Re Magi. Promossi a un livello superiore, ad esempio al ruolo di arcangeli, possono entrare nelle schiere celesti e, dall'alto delle nuvole, infilzare i démoni con le loro lance…

Da sempre questo esserino sorridente, questo infante paffuto, è stato oggetto di un culto particolare. Nelle più antiche teogonie era considerato un dio creatore, nato dal caos primitivo, e uno degli elementi primordiali del mondo. *Eros* per i greci, presiedeva ai matrimoni o alle vittorie e, dal VI secolo A.C., si cominciò a vedere in lui l'intermediario tra gli dei e gli uomini, la divinità della passione e dell'amore. Con o senza arco ha ispirato quasi tutti i poeti e gli artisti che lo dipingevano nell'atto d'infiammare i cuori o di ferirli con le sue frecce. Soprannominato *Amore* o *Cupido* dai romani, *Eros* conservò le forme infantili conferitegli da Prassitele e che i suoi successori avrebbero spinto fino a fargli assumere i tratti dell'adolescenza. Sembra che siano stati gli ebrei a fare il passo e collegare questo piccolo dio dell'amore agli angeli (dal latino *angelus* e dal greco *angelos*, che significa *messaggero*) ai quali si offriva ospitalità e che ricambiavano con benedizioni, la promessa dell'immortalità e altri benefici futuri.

A poco a poco gli angeli vennero concepiti come esseri immateriali. Si videro attribuire nomi corrispondenti alle virtù divine e alcuni geni – ad esempio i *Cherubini*, guardiani delle porte, e i *Serafini*, serpenti di fuoco alati – furono anch'essi inglobati tra gli angeli. Con l'avvento dell'era cristiana, gli angeli divennero creature incorporee, intelligenti, superiori all'anima umana. La Chiesa insegna che gli angeli sono stati creati in stato di felicità e grazia, ma con la facoltà di scegliere tra il bene e il male. Alcuni peccarono e furono perciò condannati a un supplizio che non avrà mai fine. Ci sono, così, gli *angeli buoni*, che hanno perseverato, e gli *angeli caduti*, o *angeli cattivi*, chiamati anche *diavoli* o *démoni*.

La Chiesa diffida degli angeli, molti dei quali vengono, però, menzionati nelle Scritture: Michele, Gabriele, Raffaele e, tra i cattivi: Satana, Belzebù ecc.

La tipologia dell'angelo con le ali comincia a vedersi nel IV secolo, per analogia con le figure alate note all'antichità. Non si può volerne agli artisti che, talvolta, hanno confuso gli amori con gli angeli e i serafini con i cupido… Pertanto, la loro originalità si manifesta proprio negli angeli, inizialmente nell'attitudine gerarchica, negli abiti bianchi, nell'espressione di purezza. Poi, con l'arrivo di Raffaello, il naturalismo nobile del XIII secolo (angeli di cattedrale) e la soavità vaporosa dei quattrocentisti cedettero, ben presto, il passo a una bellezza più regolare ma più pagana, in cui si ritrova l'influenza dell'antico. All'epoca del Rinascimento, si tendeva a equilibrare, come Tiziano, *amore sacro e amore profano*. Botticelli sembrò, a tutta prima, felice di dipingere da un lato Venere e dall'altro la Vergine Maria, facendo svolazzare attorno a entrambe gli stessi cherubini… Tintoretto, Veronese, Il Caravaggio narrarono soltanto di *amore vinto, amore vincitore*, mentre il Perugino esitava davanti al *Combattimento tra Amore e Castità*. Tra i fiamminghi Rubens fu quello che, in seguito, meglio riuscì a dividersi tra soggetti profani e temi sacri. Nella Francia del XVII secolo furono Poussin, poi Boucher o Fragonard a proseguire la tradizione, cedendo tanto all'amore spirituale, tanto all'amore terrestre.

Ebbene, a poco a poco, e soprattutto all'epoca dei pittori «Pompiers», l'angelo sorridente si trasformò in fantoccio di celluloide, prima di scappare, sfigurato e con le ali a brandelli, davanti alla minaccia dell'arte moderna. Oggi è scomparso, spaventato da un'epoca che ha perso il cammino del soprannaturale, cammino incantato che passava per le visioni immateriali e luminose di queste graziose creature alate. E, ciò nonostante, restiamo dipendenti da questo immaginario millenario. Da questi tesori d'arte che popolano chiese e musei. Da queste miniature innocenti conservate nelle biblioteche. Gli uomini, oggi più che mai, si sentono coinvolti nei tormenti di una lotta celeste più grande di loro: la lotta, dall'esito sempre incerto, del Bene contro il Male. In queste rappresentazioni gli angeli restano inseparabili dai démoni ai quali, da sempre, sono associati, nello spirito come nell'arte. Non sono, forse, le due facce di una stessa realtà immateriale? Non rappresentano proprio parte del risvolto onirico di una società diventata troppo materialista? «L'uomo non è né angelo né bestia» diceva nel XVII secolo Pascal. Oggi che gli angeli sono fuggiti per nascondersi, si può aggiungere, come vuole il detto popolare, che «disgrazia vuole che chi vuol fare l'angelo fa la bestia»…

José Antolínez *The Immaculate Conception of the Virgin*, 1665. Madrid, Museo del Prado

Anjos puros… Anjos radiantes…

Pintar anjos sempre agradou aos artistas, uma vez que, graças às suas pequenas asas, podemos colocá-los onde quisermos, num quadro, e de várias maneiras, se assim desejarmos. No céu, podem tocar uma variedade de instrumentos musicais, cantar e dançar. Quando crescidos, encarregam-se de levar mensagens, como anunciar à Virgem Maria que esperava um filho que viria a ser Cristo e anunciar o acontecimento dos pastorinhos ou dos Reis Magos. Chegados a um nível elevado, por exemplo, o de arcanjo, podem fazer parte da milícia celeste e, do alto das nuvens, atirar as suas lanças contra os demónios… Este pequeno ser sorridente, esta criança rechonchuda, foi sempre o objecto de um culto particular. Nas mais antigas teogonias, era considerado como um deus criador, nascido do caos primitivo e um dos elementos primordiais do mundo. Entre os Gregos chamava-se *Eros*, presidia aos casamentos ou vitórias e, a partir do século VI AC, passou a ser visto como o intermediário entre os deuses e os homens, a divindade da paixão e do amor. Com ou sem arco, inspirou quase todos os poetas e artistas que o mostraram a arrebatar os corações ou a feri-los com as suas flechas. Designado *Amor* ou *Cupido* pelos Romanos, *Eros* conservou as formas da infância que Praxíteles lhe havia concedido e que os seus sucessores possuíam até à adolescência. Parece que foram os Hebreus a dar o passo entre este pequeno deus do amor e os anjos (do latim *angelus* e do grego *angelos*, que quer dizer *mensageiro*), a quem se oferecia hospitalidade e agradecia as bênçãos, a promessa de prosperidade e outras satisfações. Pouco a pouco, os anjos foram concebidos como seres imateriais. Foram lhes dados nomes correspondentes às virtudes divinas e certos espíritos – como os *Quérubes*, guardiões das portas, e os *Serafins*, serpentes de fogo aladas – foram englobados entre os anjos. Com a chegada da era cristã, os anjos tornaram-se em substâncias incorporais, inteligentes, superiores à alma do homem. A Igreja ensina que os anjos foram criados num estado de felicidade e de graça, mas com a liberdade de escolher entre o Bem e o Mal. Alguns pecaram e foram condenados a um suplício sem fim. Existem, por isso, os *anjos bons*, os que perseveraram, e os *anjos caídos* ou *anjos maus*, aos quais chamamos igualmente de *diabos* ou *demónios*. A Igreja desconfia dos anjos, mas muitos são mencionados na Escritura: Miguel, Gabriel, Rafael e, entre os maus, Satanás, Belzebu, etc. O tipo de anjo dotado de asas começa a formar-se no século IV, por analogia com as figuras aladas que a Antiguidade conheceu. Não podemos levar a mal que os artistas tivessem confundido os Amores com os Anjos e os Serafins com os Cupidos… A originalidade manifesta-se,

Raphael Detail of *Saint Michael Slaying the Dragon* c. 1518. Paris, Musée du Louvre contudo, nos anjos, em primeiro lugar, na atitude hierática, no vestuário branco, na expressão de pureza. Depois, com o nobre naturalismo do século XIII (anjos das catedrais), a suavidade vaporosa dos quatrocentistas cedo deixou passar uma beleza mais regular, mas mais pagã, onde encontramos a influência do Antigo, quando veio Rafael. Efectivamente, na época do Renascimento, balançava-se, como Titiano Vicellio, entre *O Amor Sagrado e o Amor Profano*. Botticelli parecia totalmente feliz por pintar Vénus com uma mão e a Virgem Maria com a outra, fazendo esvoaçar no céu, à volta delas, os mesmos querubins… Tintoretto, Veronese, Caravaggio apenas falavam do *Amor Vencido, o Amor Vencedor*, enquanto que Perugino hesitava perante *O Combate do Amor e da Castidade*. De entre os Flamengos, Rubens foi o que, em seguida, melhor fez a separação entre os sujeitos profanos e os temas sagrados. Em França, no século XVII, foram Poussin, depois Boucher ou Fragonard, que trouxeram a luz, ora ao amor espiritual, ora ao amor terrestre. Infelizmente, pouco a pouco e sobretudo na época dos pintores «enfáticos», o anjo sorridente transformou-se em bebé de celulóide, antes de se desvanecer, desfigurado, com as asas despedaçadas, perante as ameaças da arte moderna. Hoje, desapareceu, intimidado por uma época que perdeu o caminho do sobrenatural, o caminho encantado que passava pelas visões imateriais e luminosas das suas graciosas criaturas aladas. Contudo, permanecemos dependentes destas imagens milenares, destes tesouros artísticos que povoam as igrejas e museus, destas iluminuras ingénuas conservadas nas bibliotecas. Os humanos sentem-se, mais do que nunca, presos no medo de um combate celeste que os ultrapassa: o combate, sempre incerto, do Bem contra o Mal. Nestas representações, os anjos permanecem inseparáveis dos demónios aos quais sempre estiveram associados, tanto nos espíritos como na arte. Não são eles as duas faces de uma mesma realidade imaterial? Não representam eles precisamente uma parte de sonho de uma sociedade tornada demasiado materialista? «O homem não é anjo nem besta», disse Pascal no século XVII. Hoje que os anjos desapareceram, é possível acrescentar, segundo o ditado popular, que «a desventura manda, infelizmente, que quem quer ser anjo acaba por ser uma besta»…

School of Provence *Jacob's Dream*. The angels climbing the mystic ladder that rises to the clouds, where a bearded figure of God the Father appears, 15th c. Avignon, Musée du Petit Palais

Love Triumphant

▲ **Egyptian artist** *Isis and Nephtys*. Belt ornament of the pharaoh from
the time of Tutankhamun, c. 1340 BC. Cairo, Egyptian Museum
◄ **The Painter of Medias** *Adonis and Aphrodite*. Detail of a red-figured
Greek vase, 410 BC. Florence, Museo Archeologico
► *Eros*. Terra-cotta in Hellenistic style. Rome, Museo Nazionale
► ► *Nike of Samothrace*. Hellenistic style of Rhodos, c. 190 BC. Paris, Musée du Louvre
► ► ► *Statuettes of Eros*. Terra-cotta from Asia Minor, second half of the 6th c. BC.
Pella, Archeological Museum

▲ *Winged Genius.* Celebrating the mysteries of Dionysus. Fresco, 50 BC. Pompeii, Villa dei Misteri
◄ *Winged Genius.* Fresco from the Villa of Publius Fannius Sinistor near Pompeii,
third quarter of the 1st c. BC. Paris, Musée du Louvre
◄◄ *Sacred Mariage.* Attic red-figured pelike in the style of Kerch,
third quarter of the 4th c. BC. Pella, Archeological Museum

Diego Velázquez *The Toilet of Venus* (detail), 1647–1651. London, National Gallery

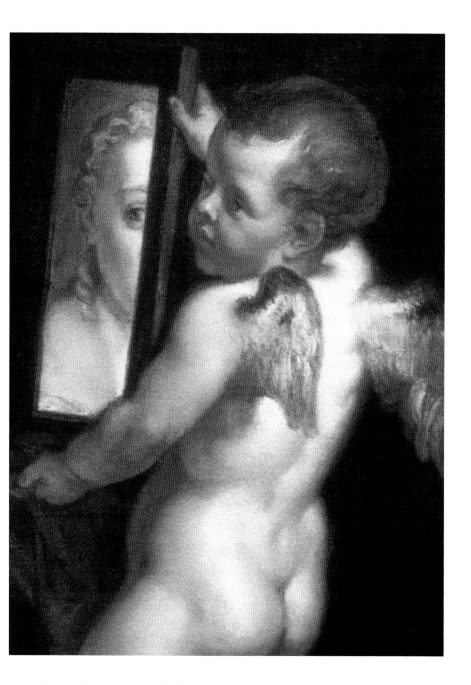

Peter Paul Rubens *Venus and Cupid* (detail), 1600–1608. Madrid, Museo Thyssen-Bornemisza

Parmigianino *Bow-Carving Amor*, c. 1533/34. Vienna, Kunsthistorisches Museum

Raphael *The Triumph of Galatea*. Fresco, c. 1511. Rome, Villa della Farnesina

▲ **Peter Paul Rubens** *The Garden of Love* (detail), c. 1633. Madrid, Museo del Prado
◄ **Lucas Cranach the Elder** *Cupid Complaining to Venus*, c. 1530. London, The National Gallery   29

Jean-Auguste-Dominique Ingres *Venus Anadyomène*, 1848. Chantilly, Musée Condé

Gustave Moreau *The Birth of Venus* (detail), c. 1880–1885. Paris, Musée Moreau

31

▲ **Jan Vermeer** *A Young Woman Standing at a Virginal* (detail), c. 1670. London, The National Gallery.
Cupid represents faithful love, but can also symbolize forbidden love.

▲ **Sandro Botticelli** *Cupid Blind-folded*. Detail of *The Spring*, c. 1481. Florence, Galleria degli Uffizi
◄◄ **Caravaggio** *Victorious Cupid*, c. 1602. Berlin, Gemäldegalerie

►► **Albrecht Altdorfer** *The Assumption of the Virgin* (detail), c. 1510–1515. Paris, Bibliothèque Nationale

In heaven the Virtues, Archangels and Angels, on earth the widows, couples and children. 35

Witwen

Eelewth

Kindler

Musicians of the Soul

▲ **Giotto di Bondone** Detail of *The Presentation in the Temple.*
Fresco, 1302–1305. Padua, Cappella degli Scrovegni (Arena Chapel)
◄ **Giotto di Bondone** Detail of *The Lamentation of Christ.*
Fresco, 1302–1305. Padua, Cappella degli Scrovegni (Arena Chapel)

Giotto di Bondone Detail of *Joachim's Dream.* Fresco, 1302–1305.
Padua, Cappella degli Scrovegni (Arena Chapel)

Carlo di Braccesco Detail of *The Annunciation*, central panel of a triptych, late 15th c.
Paris, Musée du Louvre

Giotto di Bondone Detail of *The Flight to Egypt*. Fresco, 1302–1305.
Padua, Cappella degli Scrovegni (Arena Chapel)

46   *Seraphim with Six Wings.* Detail of the Byzantine mosaic, 12th/13th c. Venice, Basilica San Marco

Angels Holding Scrolls. Detail of the mural paintings, c. 1450. Bourges, Palais Jacques-Cœur   47

Angels Carrying Pillars. Stained glass window (detail) of Notre-Dame de la Belle Verrière, c. 1180.

Chartres, cathedral

Smiling Angel. Sculpture from the west facade. c. 1245–1255. Reims, cathedral
This smile is as famous as the Mona Lisa's.

Cimabue Detail of *Madonna and Child Enthroned (Maestà di Santa Trinità)*, c. 1280–1290.
Florence, Galleria degli Uffizi

Duccio di Buoninsegna Detail of *Madonna and Child Enthroned with Six Angels (Maestà Rucellai)*, 1285. Florence, Galleria degli Uffizi

▲ **Andrea Mantegna** Detail of the fresco in the Bridal Chamber
(Camera degli Sposi), c. 1474. Mantua, Palazzo Ducale
▶ **Fra Angelico** Detail of *The Last Judgement*, 1432–1435. Florence, Museo di San Marco
◀◀ **Enguerrand Quarton** Detail of *The Coronation of the Virgin*, c. 1453.
Villeneuve-lès-Avignon, Musée de l'Hospice

▶▶ **Fra Angelico** Detail of *The Perugia Triptych*, 1437. Perugia, Galleria Nazionale dell'Umbria

▲ **Giotto di Bondone** Detail of *Madonna and Child Enthroned with Angels and Saints (Ognissanti Madonna)*, c. 1306–1310. Florence, Galleria degli Uffizi

Benvenuto di Giovanni Guasta Detail of *The Life of Mary*, c. 1470. Volterra, Pinacoteca comunale

▲ **Albrecht Altdorfer** Detail of *The Birth of the Virgin*, c. 1525. Munich, Alte Pinakothek
▶▶ **Jean de Gourmont** *Adoration of the Shepherds* (detail), c. 1525. Paris, Musée du Louvre 59

▴ **Rosso Fiorentino** Detail of *Madonna and Child with Four Saints*, 1518. Florence, Galleria degli Uffizi
◂ **Raphael** *Angel*. Fragment of *The Pala Baronci*, c. 1500/01. Brescia, Pinacoteca Civica Tosio-Martinengo 63

▲ Fra Angelico *The Archangel Gabriel* (detail), c. 1440. Museo di San Giovanni Valdarno
▶ Fra Bartolomeo *The Apparition of the Virgin to St. Bernard* (detail), 1504–1507. Florence, Galleria degli Uffizi

▲ Peter Paul Rubens *Jesus as a Child and Saint John with Two Cherubs*, c. 1618.
Vienna, Kunsthistorisches Museum
◄ Peter Paul Rubens Detail of *The Coronation of the Virgin*, c. 1618–1620. Munich, Alte Pinakothek   67

▲ **Anthony Van Dyck** Detail of *The Virgin with Partridges (The Rest on the Flight to Egypt)*, c. 1630. Florence, Palazzo Pitti

▶ **Philippe de Champaigne** Detail of *The Nativity*, 1643. Lille, Musée des Beaux-Arts

68   ▶▶ **Neapolitan artist** *Raphael the Archangel*, late 16th c. Los Angeles, County Museum of Art

▲ **Peter Paul Rubens** Detail of *The Prophet Elijah Receiving Bread and Water from an Angel*, c. 1625–1628. Bayonne, Musée Bonnat

▲ **Bartholomé Esteban Murillo** *The Angels' Kitchen* (detail), 1646. Paris, Musée du Louvre

►► **Fra Angelico** *Angels Musicians.* Detail of *The Virgin of Humility*, c. 1433–1435.
Madrid, Museo Thyssen-Bornemisza

73

▲ **Fra Angelico** Detail of *The Coronation of the Virgin*, 1434/1435. Paris, Musée du Louvre
▸ **Giotto di Bondone** Detail of *The Baroncelli Polyptych*, c. 1434–1435. Florence, Santa Croce

◄◄ **Fra Angelico** *Music-Making Angels.* Two details of *The Linaiuoli Tabernacle*, 1433.
Florence, Museo di San Marco

◄ **Stefan Lochner** Detail of *Madonna in the Rose Bower*, c. 1450. Cologne, Wallraf-Richartz-Museum

▲ **Neri di Bicci** Detail of *The Coronation of the Virgin*, 14th c. Avignon, Musée du Petit Palais   81

Fra Angelico Detail of *The Linaiuoli Tabernacle*, 1433. Florence, Museo di San Marco

Melozzo da Forlì *Music-Making Angel*, detail of a fresco, c. 1480. Rome, Pinacoteca Vaticana   83

▴ **Albrecht Dürer** Detail of *The Festival of the Rosary*, 1506. Prague, Národní Galerie
▸ **Pietro Perugino** *Music-Making Angels*. Detail of the Altarpiece for the
Abbey of Vallombrosa, 1500. Florence, Galleria dell' Accademia

▲ **Rosso Fiorentino** *Music-Making Angel,* 1521. Florence, Galleria degli Uffizi
◀ **Matthias Grünewald** Detail of *The Isenheim Altarpiece,* c. 1512–1516.
Colmar, Musée d'Unterlinden

Ridolfo Ghirlandaio Detail of *The Coronation of the Virgin*, 1504. Avignon, Musée du Petit Palais

Hubert and Jan Van Eyck *Music-Making Angels.*
Detail of *The Ghent Altarpiece*, c. 1432. Ghent, St. Baafskathedraal

Matthias Grünewald Detail of *The Isenheim Altarpiece,* c. 1512–1516. Colmar, Musée d'Unterlinden

Luca Signorelli Detail of *Virgin and Child with Saints*, c. 1483/84.
Perugia, Museo dell'Opera del Duomo

Luca Signorelli *The Angels' Concert*. Detail of *The Coronation of the Elect*, 1499–1504.

Orvieto, Duomo, Cappella di S. Brizio

Giovanni di Paolo *Five Angels Dancing Before the Sun*, 15th c. Chantilly, Musée Condé

Fra Angelico Detail of *The Last Judgement,* 1432–1435. Florence, Museo di San Marco   95

Ritual of Passover. Illumination from a Cretan manuscript of *La Haggadah,* 1583

Israfil. The Angel of Resurrection sounding the trumpet.
Detail from an Arabian manuscript, 16th c. London, British Library

Hosein Naggâsh *Raphael and the Fish*, c. 1590. Paris, Musée Guimet

Iranian artist Illumination (detail) of Nizimi's five epic poems, known as *The Khamsa*, from the Safavide period, 17th c. Paris, Bibliothèque Nationale

Divine Messengers

▲ **Fra Angelico** *The Annunciation* (detail), c. 1450. Florence, Museo di San Marco
One of 41 panels of the *Armadio degli argenti* for Santissima Annunziata in Florence.
◄ **Fra Angelico (workshop)** Fragment of the *Adoring Angel* (detail), 15th c. Paris, Musée du Louvre   101

Hubert and Jan Van Eyck *The Archangel Gabriel* from *The Annunciation.*
Detail of *The Ghent Altarpiece*, c. 1432. Ghent, St. Baafskathedraal

▲ *The Annunciation.* Illuminated initial from a Missal, 15th c. Florence, Museo di San Marco

►► **Melozzo da Forli** (?) *Annunciating Angel,* c. 1466–1470. Florence, Galleria degli Uffizi 103

▸ *The Archangel Gabriel* from *The Annunciation*. Miniature from the
Heures de Charles de France, 1465. New York, Metropolitan Museum of Art

▲ **Fra Angelico** Detail of *The Perugia Triptych*, 1437. Perugia, Galleria Nazionale dell'Umbria
◄ **Rogier Van der Weyden** *Angel* from *The Annunciation* (detail), c. 1440 (?). Paris, Musée du Louvre   107

Leonardo da Vinci *The Annunciation* (detail), c. 1472. Florence, Galleria degli Uffizi

▲ **Domenico Ghirlandaio** Detail of *The Adoration of the Magi*, 1488.
Florence, Galleria dell'Ospedale degli Innocenti
▸ **Gian Lorenzo Bernini** *The Ecstasy of Saint Theresa*. Marble, 1645–1652.
Rome, Santa Maria della Vittoria

▲ **Sandro Botticelli** *The Annunciation* (detail), c. 1489. Florence, Galleria degli Uffizi
◄ **Filippino Lippi** Detail of *The Vision of Saint Bernard*, 1480s. Fiesole, Badia Fiesolana
▶▶ **Mathieu Le Nain** *The Annunciation*, 17th c. Autun, Musée Rolin

▸ **Domenico Ghirlandaio** Detail of *Madonna and Child, Angels and Saints*, c. 1484–1486.

Florence, Galleria degli Uffizi

▲ Andrea del Sarto *The Annunciation* (detail), 1512. Florence, Palazzo Pitti
◄ Matthias Grünewald *The Isenheim Altarpiece* (detail), c. 1512–1516. Colmar, Musée d'Unterlinden   117

▲ **Domenico Ghirlandaio** Detail of *The Christ in Glory*, 1492. Volterra, Pinacoteca Comunale
▸ **Hugo van der Goes** Detail of *The Nativity*. Central panel of *The Portinari Altarpiece*, c. 1475.
Florence, Galleria degli Uffizi

▲ **Cimabue** *The Virgin and Child Enthroned Surrounded by Angels,* c. 1270. Paris, Musée du Louvre

◄◄ **Andrea del Sarto** *The Assumption of the Virgin* (detail), c. 1520. Florence, Palazzo Pitti

Giotto di Bondone *Madonna and Child Enthroned with Angels and Saints (Ognissanti Madonna)*, c. 1306–1310. Florence, Galleria degli Uffizi

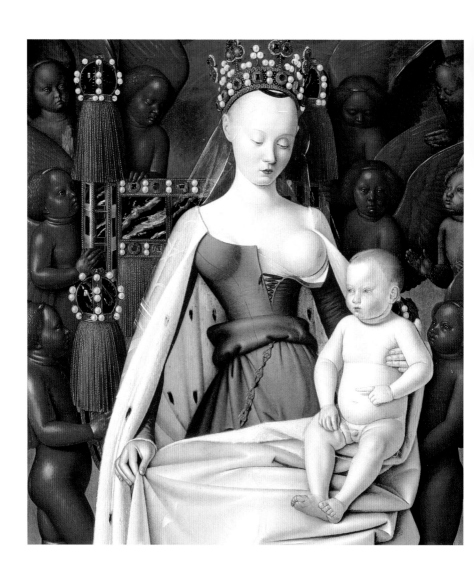

Jean Fouquet *Madonna and Child*. Right wing of *The Melun Diptych,* c. 1456.
Antwerp, Koninklijk Museum voor Schone Kunsten

Raphael *The Sistine Madonna*, c. 1513/14. Dresden, Gemäldegalerie Alte Meister 125

▲ Peter Paul Rubens *Virgin and Child Surrounded by Angels* (detail), c. 1618. Paris, Musée du Louvre
◄ El Greco Detail of *The Assumption of the Virgin*, c. 1610–1614. Toledo, Museo de Santa Cruz
►► Frans Francken the Younger and Abraham Govaerts *Madonna and Child in a Landscape.*
Surrounded by angels making music and dancing, early 17th c. Lyon, Musée des Beaux-Arts 127

▲ Peter Paul Rubens *Annunciation*, 1609–1610. Vienna, Kunsthistorisches Museum
▶ Annibale Caracci (**workshop**) *The Translation of the Holy House* (detail), early 17th c.
Rome, San Onofrio, Cappella Madruzzo

▲ **William Bouguereau** *The Virgin with Angels*, 1900. Paris, Musée du Petit Palais
◄ **Evelyn de Morgan** *Our Lady of Peace*, 1907. London, The De Morgan Foundation   133

The Baptism of Christ. Miniature from the *Très Belles Heures de Notre-Dame du duc de Berry,*
c. 1404–1409. Paris, Bibliothèque Nationale

Francisco de Goya *Christ on the Mount of Olives* (detail), c. 1810–1819. Paris, Musée du Louvre

Jacques de Stella *Christ Served by the Angels*, 17ᵗʰ c. Florence, Galleria degli Uffizi

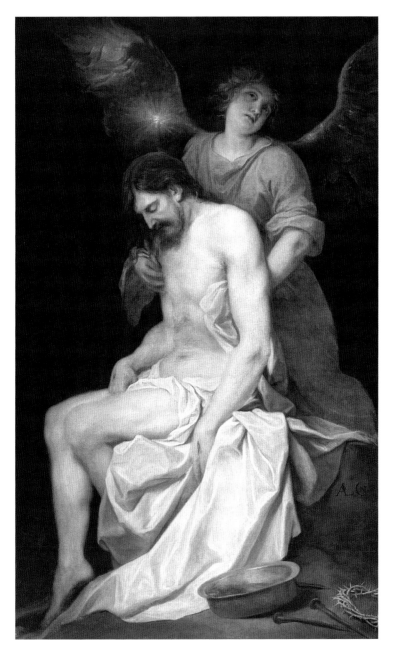

▲ **Alonso Cano** *Dead Christ Supported by an Angel*, c. 1646–1652. Madrid, Museo del Prado

◄ **Antonello da Messina** *Dead Christ Sustained by an Angel*, c. 1476. Madrid, Museo del Prado   139

▲ *Dead Christ.* Miniature from the *Très Belles Heures de Notre-Dame du Duc de Berry,* c. 1404–1409.

► **Giotto** *The Lamentation of Christ* (detail). Fresco, 1302–1305. Padua, Cappella degli Scrovegni

EGO VERI
SVM TAS ET
VIA VITA

The Celestial Armies

▲ *The Seventh Angel of the Apocalypse Proclaiming the Reign of the Lord.*
Detail of a Spanish manuscript, c. 1180. New York, Metropolitan Museum of Art
◀ *Christ's Soldier*. Detail of a Byzantine mosaic, c. 520. Ravenna, Museo Arcivescovile   143

▲ *The Mission of the Seven Angels with the Seven Goblets.* Detail of a Spanish manuscript of Beatus de Liébana's *Commentaries on the Apocalypse*, 1091–1109. Madrid, Biblioteca Nazionale

▸ **Guariento di Arpo** (?) *The Celestial Army* (detail), 1378. Padua, Museo Civico

Warrior Angel. Detail of a stained glass window, c. 1180. Chartres, cathedral

The Warrior Angels. Detail of a mosaic, mid 13th c. Florence, Battistero San Giovanni

Théophanie: Adoration of God in Heaven.
Detail of a Spanish manuscript of Beatus de Liébana's *Commentaries on the Apocalypse*, c. 1180.

El Escorial, Real Biblioteca de San Lorenzo

The Sixth Angel Delivers the Four Angels Enchained in the Euphrates.
From a Spanish manuscript of Beatus de Liébana's *Commentaries on the Apocalypse*, c. 1180.
New York, Metropolitan Museum of Art

▲ *Gabriel* from *the Annunciation* (detail), early 12th c. (?). Ohrid, Eglise de la Vierge Péribleptos

◄ **Guariento di Arpo** *Angel in Battle Dress*, 1354. Padua, Museo Civico

▲ Bernardino Zenale *Saint Michael the Archangel*, c. 1490. Florence, Galleria degli Uffizi

▸ **French or English School** (**?**) *The Wilton Diptych* (detail), c. 1395–1399. London, National Gallery

Paciano di Bonaguida *The Apparition of Saint Michael*. Miniature from an
illuminated Italian manuscript, c. 1340. London, The British Library

The Limburg Brothers *Saint Michael's Fight with the Dragon.* Miniature from the
Très Riches Heures du Duc de Berry, c. 1410–1416. Chantilly, Musée Condé

▲ **Antonio del Pollaiolo** *The Archangel Michael*, c. 1475. Florence, Museo Bardini

▸ **Raphael** *Saint Michael Slaying the Dragon* (detail), c. 1518. Paris, Musée du Louvre

▸▸ Pieter Bruegel the Elder *The Fall of the Rebel Angels* (detail), 1562.
Brussels, Musées royaux des Beaux-Arts

Frans Floris *The Fall of the Rebel Angels* (detail), c. 1600.
Antwerp, Koninklijk Museum voor Schone Kunsten

The Limburg Brothers *The Fall of the Rebel Angels.* Miniature from the
Très Riches Heures du Duc de Berry, c. 1410–1416. Chantilly, Musée Condé

The Battle in Paradise. Miniature from
an illuminated manuscript of Beatus de
Liébana's *Commentaries on the Apocalypse*, c.
1320. New York, Metropolitan Museum of Art

Francesco Botticini *The Three Archangels with Tobias*, c. 1470.
Florence, Galleria degli Uffizi

Rogier Van der Weyden *The Elect Entering Paradise.*
Detail of *The Last Judgement*, c. 1450. Beaune, Musée Hôtel-Dieu   165

▲ Dieric Bouts *The Way to Paradise* (detail), c. 1450. Lille, Musée des Beaux-Arts
◄ Hans Memling *Judgement and Weighing of Souls* (detail), 1480. Gdansk, Muzeum Narodowe   169

▲ **Lucas Cranach the Elder** *The Trinity*, c. 1518 (?). Leipzig, Museum der Bildenden Künste
◄ *Adoration of God the Father*. Miniature from the T*rès Belles Heures du Duc de Berry*, c. 1404–1409

Rembrandt van Rijn *The Ascension of Christ*, c. 1636. Munich, Alte Pinakothek

▴ **Giotto di Bondone** *Christ in Glory*. Detail of *The Last Judgement*. Fresco, 1302–1305.
Padua, Cappella degli Scrovegni (Arena Chapel)

▸▸ **Master of the Holy Kinship** *Christ Appears to His Mother*. c. 1480. Paris, Musée du Louvre 173

▲ **Stefan Lochner** *Madonna in the Rose Bower*, c. 1450. Cologne, Wallraf-Richartz-Museum
◄ *The Coronation of the Virgin*. Miniature, late 15ᵗʰ c. Paris, Bibliothèque Nationale

Flemish School *The Angels' Concert*. Detail of *The Virgin in Glory*, 15th c.
Bilbao, Museo de Bellas Artes

The Crowned Virgin Appears to a Donor in Prayer. Miniature from the
Heures dites de Baudricourt, c. 1470. Paris, Bibliothèque Nationale

180 **Peter Paul Rubens** *The Assumption of the Virgin* (detail), c. 1614. Vienna, Kunsthistorisches Museum

Titian *The Assumption of the Virgin* (detail), 1516–1518. Venice, Santa Maria Gloriosa dei Frari   181

Bartolomé Esteban Murillo *The Immaculate Conception* (detail), c. 1678.
Madrid, Museo del Prado

Guido Reni *The Assumption of the Virgin*, 1631/1642. Munich, Alte Pinakothek

Bernardo Cavallino *The Immaculate Conception* (detail), 17th c. Milan, Pinacoteca di Brera

José Antolínez *The Assumption of Mary Magdalene*, 1670–1675. Madrid, Museo del Prado 185

Master of Moulins *The Coronation of the Virgin*. Central panel of the triptych of
The Virgin in Glory, 1498–1501. Moulins, cathedral

Matthew the Evangelist. Miniature from the *Heures de Rivoire*, c. 1465–1470.

Paris, Bibliothèque Nationale

Cover:
Master of the Housebook *Three Angels*. Fragment of an altarpiece, 1491. Basle, Kunstmuseum
Photo: Artothek / Hans Hinz

Frontispiece:
Gustave Moreau *Voice of the Evening*. Music-playing angels, who bring peace
with the stars of the night. Watercolour, 1884. Paris, Musée Moreau

Acknowledgements & Credits:
The publishers wish to thank the copyright holders who greatly assisted in this publication. In addition
to those persons and institutions cited in the captions, the following should also be mentioned:
© akg-images, Berlin: 11, 62, 85, 125, 130, 171, 168 (photo: Erich Lessing), 180, 33
(photo: Nimatallah); © Artothek, Weilheim: 183, 59 (photo: Joachim Blauel), 66, 80, 172, 177, 44
(photo: Hans Hinz), 116, 7 (photo: Joseph S. Martin), 29, 86, 90, 139, 26 (photo: Photobusiness),
84 (photo: Jochen Remmer), 187, 186 (photo: Peter Willi); © Bridgeman Art Library, London:
24, 25, 32, 43, 67, 68, 89, 97, 102, 114, 126, 132, 136/137, 146, 152, 153, 165, 167, 178, 182, 185, 52/53 (photo:
Giraudon), 158/159, 160, 188/189; © Museo Thyssen Bornemisza, Madrid: 74/75; © RMN, Paris:
98 (photo: Arnaudet), 127, 135, 76 (photo: J. G. Berizzi), 169, 69 (photo: P. Bernard), 41 (photo:
Gérard Blot), 72/73, 106, 30 (photo: Harry Bréjat), 60/61, 94, 133 (photo: Bulloz), 22 (photo:
Chuzeville), 31 (photo: Jean), 122 (photo: Lewandowski), 2 (photo: Ojeda), 15, 71, 88, 100, 155, 161,
13 (photo: Ojeda/Néri), 157, 81 (photo: Raux), 174 (photo: Schormans); © Scala, Florence: 27
(photo: 1990), 38, 39, 40, 42, 49, 64, 83, 91, 110, 141, 151, 156, 173, 175, 181, 184, 50 (photo: 1994), 138,
118 (photo 1996), 147 (photo: 1997), 92/93 (photo: 2000), 23 (Courtesy of the Ministero Beni e
Att. Culturali – © 1990), 51, 55, 56, 77, 78, 79, 82, 87, 95, 101, 103 104, 107, 111, 115, 117, 119, 120/121,
164, 34/35 (© 1991), 57, 123, 63 (© 1996); © The Uffizi, Florence: 4, 8, 65, 113, 108/109.

To stay informed about upcoming TASCHEN titles,
please request our magazine at www.taschen.com or write to
TASCHEN, Hohenzollernring 53, D–50672 Cologne, Germany, Fax: +49-221-254919.
We will be happy to send you a free copy of our magazine which is filled
with information about all of our books.

© 2004 TASCHEN GmbH
Hohenzollernring 53, D–50672 Köln
www.taschen.com

Text and layout: Gilles Néret, Paris
Editorial coordination: Annick Volk, Cologne
Picture research: Ines Dickmann, Cologne
Production: Thomas Grell, Cologne
Spanish translation: Gemma Deza Guil for LocTeam, S.L., Barcelona
Italian translation: Adriana Esposito for LocTeam, S.L., Barcelona
Portuguese translation: Vanessa Marques for LocTeam, S.L., Barcelona

Printed in Italy
ISBN 3–8228–2984–6

What Great Paintings Say I
Rose-Marie & Rainer Hagen
Flexi-cover, 496 pp. / € 29.99/
$ 39.99 / £ 19.99 / ¥ 5.900

What Great Paintings Say II
Rose-Marie & Rainer Hagen
Flexi-cover, 432 pp. / € 29.99/
$ 39.99 / £ 19.99 / ¥ 5.900

Devils
Gilles Néret / Flexi-cover, Icons,
192 pp. / € 6.99 / $ 9.99 /
£ 4.99 / ¥ 1.500

"These books are beautiful objects, well-designed and lucid." —*Le Monde*, Paris, on the ICONS series

"Buy them all and add some pleasure to your life."

Alchemy & Mysticism
Alexander Roob

All-American Ads 40ˢ
Ed. Jim Heimann

All-American Ads 50ˢ
Ed. Jim Heimann

All-American Ads 60ˢ
Ed. Jim Heimann

Angels
Gilles Néret

Architecture Now!
Ed. Philip Jodidio

Art Now
Eds. Burkhard Riemschneider,
Uta Grosenick

Berlin Style
Ed. Angelika Taschen

Chairs
Charlotte & Peter Fiell

Design of the 20ᵗʰ Century
Charlotte & Peter Fiell

Design for the 21ˢᵗ Century
Charlotte & Peter Fiell

Devils
Gilles Néret

Digital Beauties
Ed. Julius Wiedemann

Robert Doisneau
Ed. Jean-Claude Gautrand

East German Design
Ralf Ulrich / Photos: Ernst
Hedler

Egypt Style
Ed. Angelika Taschen

M.C. Escher

Fashion
Ed. The Kyoto Costume
Institute

HR Giger
HR Giger

Grand Tour
Harry Seidler,
Ed. Peter Gössel

Graphic Design
Ed. Charlotte & Peter Fiell

Havana Style
Ed. Angelika Taschen

Homo Art
Gilles Néret

Hot Rods
Ed. Coco Shinomiya

Hula
Ed. Jim Heimann

India Bazaar
Samantha Harrison,
Bari Kumar

Industrial Design
Charlotte & Peter Fiell

Japanese Beauties
Ed. Alex Gross

Kitchen Kitsch
Ed. Jim Heimann

Krazy Kids' Food
Eds. Steve Roden,
Dan Goodsell

Las Vegas
Ed. Jim Heimann

Mexicana
Ed. Jim Heimann

Mexico Style
Ed. Angelika Taschen

Morocco Style
Ed. Angelika Taschen

**Extra/Ordinary Objects,
Vol. I**
Ed. Colors Magazine

**Extra/Ordinary Objects,
Vol. II**
Ed. Colors Magazine

Paris Style
Ed. Angelika Taschen

Penguin
Frans Lanting

20ᵗʰ Century Photography
Museum Ludwig Cologne

Pin-Ups
Ed. Burkhard Riemschneider

Provence Style
Ed. Angelika Taschen

Pussycats
Gilles Néret

Safari Style
Ed. Angelika Taschen

Seaside Style
Ed. Angelika Taschen

Albertus Seba. Butterflies
Irmgard Müsch

**Albertus Seba. Shells &
Corals**
Irmgard Müsch

Starck
Ed Mae Cooper, Pierre Doze,
Elisabeth Laville

Surfing
Ed. Jim Heimann

Sydney Style
Ed. Angelika Taschen

Tattoos
Ed. Henk Schiffmacher

Tiffany
Jacob Baal-Teshuva

Tiki Style
Sven Kirsten

Tuscany Style
Ed. Angelika Taschen

Women Artists
in the 20ᵗʰ and 21ˢᵗ Century
Ed. Uta Grosenick